Happy Families

Happy Families

A Parents' Guide to the Non-Violent Resistance Approach

CARMELITE AVRAHAM-KREHWINKEL
and DAVID ALDRIDGE

Jessica Kingsley Publishers
London and Philadelphia

First published in 2010
by Jessica Kingsley Publishers
116 Pentonville Road
London N1 9JB, UK
and
400 Market Street, Suite 400
Philadelphia, PA 19106, USA

www.jkp.com

Library of Congress Cataloging in Publication Data
A CIP catalog record for this book is available from the Library of Congress

British Library Cataloguing in Publication Data
A CIP catalogue record for this book is available from the British Library

ISBN 978 1 84905 084 5

Printed and bound in the United States by
Thomson-Shore, 7300 Joy Road, Dexter, MI 48130

Dedicated to my children and my inspiration,
David and Jonathan
Carmelite Avraham-Krehwinkel

Dedicated to
Emily, Luc, Nadine, and their children,
Jessica, Bluebell, Molly, Poppy, Honey, Gabriel* and Sophie*
David Aldridge

* in memoriam

Contents

Acknowledgements

In the long process of bringing this book to its completion, we were privileged to have had the help of many colleagues and friends.

We would like first to express our gratitude to the many families who shared with us their story and trusted us in the process to initiate change and stability in their lives.

Our thanks go to the many students who worked with dedication on this project, in particular, Naama Gershi, Assaf Wexler and Gil Ilani.

Special thanks are extended to Dr Gil Gilad from the Behavioural Science Department, Academic College of Tel-Aviv Jaffa, for bringing his expertise and experience to bear on the processing and analysis of the data.

This book has been conceived, developed, discussed and written in three languages: Hebrew, English and German. We would therefore like to thank the following people for their dedicated and invaluable help: Tova Faust, Barbara Kempinski and Christine Müllender.

Special thanks are extended to Sarah Malka Eisen for her excellent and committed work in editing the manuscript.

We would like to thank, Professor Dr Lutz Neugebauer, Co-Director of the Nordoff Robbins Center in Witten, Germany, for his continuing encouragement.

Last but not least, our thanks go to Anati Hoffner-Raccah and Dr Yigal Hoffner from Shenkar College of Engineering and Design for their moral, technical and editorial support throughout this work.

Note

All names of patients and their families have been changed.

What is Non-Violent Resistance?

You come home late from work. The kids have to be fed. You have forgotten how many other things you have to do. On the kitchen table is a note from your child's school saying he has been excluded from lessons. You can find him easily enough. Just follow the noise. But can you get into his room to see him? The door is locked and when you try and reason with him, he shouts and swears. Things are getting worse. Even though he is now excluded from school, he has been skipping lessons anyway.

As a teacher, you may have been relieved that he is not in your classroom any more. Even thinking about his presence brings on that sinking feeling in the pit of your stomach. Not another disrupted lesson. But the relief is also mixed with a sense of failure. As parent and teacher you share the same emotions of failure, frustration and helplessness. The child too.

This book is about how to get out of the situation where everyone thinks that they have failed by taking steps to regain competence. We assume that each one of you has tried to do your best. Nobody gets up each day thinking, 'How can I do my worst?' As parents and teachers we have to regain our moral authority. What a shockingly old-fashioned concept in a modern world. But that is the step we have to take. We are responsible for the child. Every child has the right to hear the word 'no' as well as 'yes'.

Throughout the western world we are hearing different variations of the same problem. Children are increasingly violent with their parents and teachers. Families are disrupted and increasing numbers of children and teenagers are being denied access to school or are themselves refusing to be educated. Children and their parents are distressed and this spreads out to friends and family.

We have written this book because there is an urgent need for a realistic, practical and efficient approach that parents, and teachers, can use with children who are behaving badly. It is a complex problem and all the research shows that once your child is behaving really badly then it is harder to do anything about it. But it's not impossible. So here is a sturdy set of ways to start improving the situation.

What is Non-Violent Resistance?

Non-Violent Resistance is a tool which enables parents to block a child's destructive behaviour without inviting escalation, helping ultimately to create an atmosphere at home conducive to the expression of love and affection. Non-Violent Resistance is defined as a series of actions that impart to the child the parent's message of, 'I am not willing to continue living like this and I will do everything, short of attacking you verbally or physically, to stop this situation.'

The characteristics of Non-Violent Resistance

- Insisting with determination upon demands deemed right and important.

- Attempting vigorously to obstruct the child's destructive behaviours.

- Avoiding categorically any use of physically or verbally aggressive behaviour, such as hitting, cursing, blaming, threatening or humiliating the child.

The approach affords you as parents a moral and practical basis for demonstrating parental presence and for monitoring your child's activities. It enables you to minimize and ultimately prevent escalation.

Based on the notion that solid parental presence is the cornerstone of good relations between parent and child, the purpose of Non-Violent Resistance is to restore parental presence. As parents, the authority you are striving to achieve cannot be based on your being physically stronger than your child. It can only be based on a deep resolve to be with him and beside him. As you enhance your parental presence, it will become more likely that your child will eschew escalating patterns in favour of dialogue. Dialogue in turn becomes the basis of your mutual relationship.

Your number one priority is to meet the needs of your child. The Non-Violent Resistance approach allows for the possibility of the child's resistance to what you are doing, or even his absence from your discussions, without doing him any harm.

Foundations of the approach

The basis for the ideas in this book is the ethical stance found in the Non-Violent Resistance Movement. The advocates of Non-Violent Resistance were Mahatma Gandhi and Martin Luther King. The main principles are:

- to avoid violent reactions

- to realize that a continued struggle may be necessary

- to say exactly why we are struggling and what for

- to ask for help from family, friends and people we know well

- to take unconditional reconciliatory action by stopping blame and making peace with each other.

In basic terms, we expect that any struggle over dominance in the family will end. As parents you are responsible for your child. You decide in the best interests of your child. It is important to remember that we are talking about situations that have deteriorated into severe difficulties, including aggression. If you have surrendered to your child's demands, it may well aggravate and amplify your child's aggression. The result can be apathy or shouting matches that we as parents regret. What we want to avoid is a vicious cycle of action and reaction, with each side blaming the other. Such a vicious cycle can lead to feelings of helplessness, confusion, guilt, and anxiety for everyone involved. Helplessness is corrosive. This book is about the first steps to becoming effective as a parent.

The Non-Violent Resistance mindset

A significant first step is that we stop blaming the child. And yes, we know it is not easy. We intend to help you restore your autonomy, authority and legitimacy as a parent. Your child needs you as a parent so that he can develop himself.

A major attitude it is important for the parents to adopt here is to be consistent, and to recognize it is a struggle with the child. Parents are encouraged not to flip between one strategy or tactic and another. We have to set reasonable achievable goals for ourselves, as well as making reasonable demands of the child, without backing down. At the same time, we have to be committed to the self-restraint required to achieve our goals. To achieve this, we have to show unity with our partners in our parenting, regardless of any problematic interpersonal issues. We need to be patient, persevere and endure. That is why we will also need help and support from our friends and family.

Does it work?

The ideas we express here are not speculation. This book is based on a three-year piece of in-depth research. An example of the approach in practice is given in the case of Thomas at the end of the book. The aim of our approach is to enable and empower you as parents to cope with your child's disruptive behaviour. Our research showed that when parents applied this approach they experienced a reduction in their sense of helplessness. As parents they felt they were more effective in handling their child, and there were fewer incidents where matters were spiralling out of control. But, even more important than this, parents felt they could have authority as parents without being authoritarian or permissive. Parents felt more affection for their child and appreciated the support that they were getting.

We saw people making progress because families used their own resources. This approach is about getting you to do what you can do best and finding your own ways of dealing with situations that work for your child or children. Women particularly felt empowered.

Things changed for the better. There was less distress. Nobody was blamed as a useless parent or a bad child. Our approach is to enlist you as parents to decide what you can do for the good of your child. Sometimes, as parents, we act like photographers – we develop the negatives. Here we finish off that process and show the positives. Change happens when we have the resources to adapt and we have those within our families, friends and communities. Learning how to ask for help is also a small but significant step. It does not make us helpless; it makes us effective.

It's a start!

This is a short-term approach. It's a practical way of helping us as parents to find our feet again. Imagine your family car runs off an icy road on a snowy winter's day. Some people would try and turn the family car into a four-wheel drive all-terrain vehicle, even if it is really a family saloon. Some people would try and make it so that it never snows again in winter. Our approach is to give you just enough traction that you can get back on the road again to continue your journey. It will involve you pushing in the same direction, deciding who is in the driving seat, listening to when it is necessary to 'shove', and maybe taking a little advice about handling difficult conditions. It requires, above all, tolerance and resilience. These are qualities that we can all demonstrate and enjoy, from the stock of our human resources. You may need a little practice but you can do it.

This book will give you some tried and trusted ways to help yourselves. Think of it as a tool kit. You know the job that needs to be done. Here are the tools to help you do that job. Yes, it will be a struggle, but if you are reading this book, you know that already. Remember the work is based on the attitude of Martin Luther-King and the catchphrase at that time was, 'we shall overcome'. And you will.

Note

The word 'child' is used to describe children of both genders. For reasons of convenience, both boys and girls are referred to using the pronouns 'he' and 'him'.

Many of the statements found here are based on the results of a larger research project which, amongst other factors, tested to what extent the gender role influenced the success of the intervention. The test was designed to examine possible differential benefits of the intervention for male and female subjects.

Chapter 1

Avoiding Escalation

The problem: 'I am the boss!'

The phenomenon of children or adolescents whose patterns of behaviour are typically disruptive poses a tough challenge for parents and professionals alike. An increased tendency to argue, a lack of boundaries, expressing anger and making threats, are all part of the long list of characteristics which tend to be used to describe such children. Common to all these behaviours is the uncompromizing stand – 'I am the boss!' This statement encapsulates the defining characteristic of the defiant, non-compliant child.

As parents you soon learn that your existing repertoire of coping methods, including suggestions given to you by professionals, is not sufficient to satisfactorily deal with the problem. Your experience shows that your admonitions, yells, threats and punishments perpetuate, and at times even worsen, your child's behaviour. On the other hand, appeasing him only serves to increase his demands. Under such conditions, the home meant to be a haven becomes a battlefield with parents and children perennially engaged. The potential for escalation lurks within each fragmentary argument and divisive encounter. In this situation, as war-weary parents we often find ourselves on the verge of exhaustion, ready to retreat.

It is no wonder then that some of us, aching for a little peace and quiet, find ourselves ready to declare defeat. Yet experience shows that the relief that comes through surrender is all too brief. It is quickly followed by increased demands from the child. This self-nourishing process gains its own momentum and strength, leaving us as parents feeling as if they we have come to a dead end. We have become unwilling partners in a vicious cycle.

In this cycle, escalation comes to dictate almost all courses of action, both the parents' and the child's.

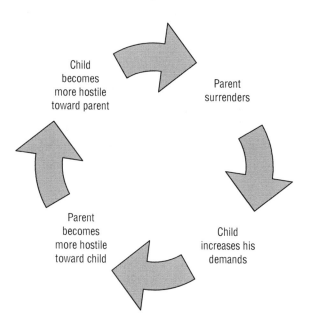

Figure 1 Escalation: The impact of power struggles on parent–child relations

Escalation

It is possible to distinguish between two types of escalation:

1. *Escalation of hostility*: This is when hostility breeds further hostility. The child begins to threaten, scream, go wild, or becomes physically aggressive when his demands are not met, and as parents we then try to impose our authority forcibly. Unfortunately, this response encourages the child's behaviour to become even more extreme.

2. *Escalation of demands*: As parents submit, the child steps up his demands and his aggression. By giving in, the parent is transmitting a weak image to the child – that we are unable to manage our child's or our own outbursts. The child then gains confidence in using threats or violence to get his own way.

These two types of escalation feed on each other. The more we yield as parents, the more we become angry, frustrated and prone to outbursts. Yet, as the then mutual outbursts become more severe, they also become more frightening, pushing us to the point where we feel ready to surrender. In this atmosphere of ongoing, intensifying escalation, it is no wonder that as parents we feel less and less able to express or sense our love for our child.

Avoiding escalation

In order to avoid escalation and in order to construct a new relationship between you and your child free of endless power struggles, you must avoid entering into conflict with him. Your child, whose control over the situation is fed by threats and violence, will continually invite you into confrontation, hoping thereby to gain the upper hand. There is a simple reason for all of this: the aggressive child 'gains' by conflict, even when he does not come out 'on top'. Just the fact that he has rattled you or made you lose control will justify his continuing extreme behaviour. This pattern does not stem from your child being inherently 'bad', but from his having developed patterns of escalation. When he does not get his way he simply escalates his behaviour.

The principle of 'not being drawn in'

You too, in all probability, have your own patterns of escalation. You too may have a kind of short fuse that prevents you from staying calm during disputes, causing you to lose control. Parents who cannot abstain from getting involved in confrontations with their children may become verbose, preachy and argumentative, using threats and shouting when dealing with their child, for example, which ultimately leads to escalation.

A typical dialogue of escalation

Parent: You are not going!

Child: Yes I am!

Parent: I said, you're not going!

Child: You can't tell me what to do!

Parent: So long as you live in this house, you will follow the house rules!

Child: I don't have to ask you! (*Slams the door*)

In the end, the child does what he wants, leaving you angry and exhausted. Escalation has occurred.

The more you attempt to explain things to, convince, preach to, and argue with your child, the more he will disregard or ignore you. Threats such as 'If…then…' will lead the child to threaten you in return. Therefore, the more you talk, the more helpless you feel. Talking less and imposing restrictions without explanation is what we call the principle of 'not being drawn in'.

TIP: Over-speaking is escalatory – it creates a feeling of helplessness. A clear restriction is more effective than explaining, preaching or trying to convince.

The principle of 'pause and postpone'

The principle of 'not being drawn in' is accompanied by the 'pause and postpone' principle. Parents typically think, 'I must immediately respond to my child's every statement, complaint or provocation.' This is fundamentally wrong. You do not need to respond to everything. Instead you should practise delaying or postponing your response. When in doubt, stay silent, rather than responding immediately. Maintaining silence is time gained, when your child wastes his ammunition, and his negative behaviours do not get a negative response from you.

TIP: Take time in planning your response to your child's demands. Remember, silence is not the same as surrender.

If you wish, you may precede your silence with a few choice words, such as 'I do not like this, and I am going to think about it.' You must say it without any hint of a threat, merely as a statement of fact. After you have repeated this strategy a number of times, your child will come to understand that your silence is not the end of the matter. Silence without surrender is more powerful than preaching or arguing. Your child will not interpret your silence as a sign of weakness, to be taken advantage of. On the contrary, our silence announces our unwillingness to accept our child's invitations to confrontation, and our desire for new avenues of communication without resorting to sermons or force.

It is important to emphasize that constructive silence should not be mistaken for detachment. Parental presence is not compromized by silence, but enhanced by it. We are proving to ourselves and to our child that we have the strength not to be drawn into conflicts. We are positioning ourselves independently as parents. Let the principles of 'not being drawn in' and 'pause and postpone', guide you when you seek to defuse episodes of escalation between you and your child.

TIP: Repeat to yourself silently when pressed: 'I will not be drawn into conflict, I will not be drawn into conflict, I will not be drawn into conflict.'

The posture of 'absorption'

The emotional posture expressed through the dual principles of 'not being drawn in' and 'pause and postpone' is 'absorption'. 'Absorption' is your readiness to absorb the child's difficult behaviour while remaining firm in the course of your conflict with him, without capitulating to the child's demands.

All in all, 'absorption' manifests the main properties of Non-Violent Resistance as listed below:

1. Courageous and unwavering stand on the central issues, where all the parent's capabilities and resources are mobilized towards frustrating the child's destructive challenges.

2. Absolute rejection of verbal or physical violence against the child, such as hitting, cursing, threatening and humiliating.

3. Resolute stance of determined struggle against violence and destructive behaviour on the one hand, coupled with a demonstrated respect for the child on the other.

4. Search to find a solution through which the child will not feel humiliated or defeated.

5. Ongoing gestures of reconciliation offered that are in no way conditional on the child's behaviour or positive change.

'Absorption' allows your child's attacks to dissolve naturally. The posture of 'absorption' addresses the two difficult emotions that invite surrender or escalation: frustration and rage. Frustration is the emotion which causes us as parents to raise our hands in surrender, preferring to buy peace and quiet through acquiescence. Rage is the emotion which leads us to try to get back at our child, using the child's own strategies in our turn. 'Absorption' allows us to maintain Non-Violent Resistance while avoiding both escalation and surrender. Putting the dual principles of 'not being drawn in' and 'pause and postpone' to use is the key for the success of the process called the 'sit-in' (which we discuss in more detail in Chapter 3) that follows the 'declaration' or 'statement of intent'.

Chapter 2

The Declaration or Statement of Intent

The declaration should voice your position, your intention and your future moves. The central component is a statement regarding your intention that all future action will be transparent, so your child, family and friends are always aware of what is happening. This future action also includes an appeal to all possible sources of future support – namely, friends and family. From this point of view, the declaration is seen as the turning point in the lives of those who have a vested interest in the process of improving your child's behaviour. You have now made a commitment to yourself, to your child, to your partner, and to the process itself.

It is a good idea to inform your child, in advance, of your unequivocal decision to share the situation with those around you, and thereby end your isolation. Telling your child in advance helps to dispel any subsequent feeling that you have acted behind his back, that you have 'turned him in' or 'betrayed' him. Knowing we have done all we can to inform our child about our plans enables us to counter accusations of this sort, and also affords us a sense of moral fortitude in continuing our struggle.

TIP: Informing your child should be done in a simple and practical manner, using no intimidation.

Timing your declaration

As a parent, you do not feel in control of your child's behaviour. You are now ready to declare your intentions, to take a stand and to take some time to reflect on your changed position. Pick a convenient time – long after a violent outburst – and announce your declaration in a calm, resolute, non-intimidating tone of voice. You should send out a message that the die has been cast, that you now stand resolved and united with your partner.

TIP: Should you fear a violent reaction from your child, consider having a third party present. The presence of others significantly reduces, and most of the time even eliminates, the occurrence of violence.

If, for any reason, you cannot communicate directly with your child, ask a mediator to bring your written declaration to the child. A mediator is a person who is capable of bridging the gap between you and your child by communicating your concerns to him, and the child's concerns to you. He or she should be a person with whom your child is willing to talk. It can be a friend, a relative, a teacher or any other person with whom your child is acquainted. Your job is to find a mediator and to be willing to share your situation with him or her, even when it is not flattering. Declarations should always be made orally and in writing. Even when you have already made your announcement and your child has heard you speak, the written word adds conviction, empowering both word and action.

TIP: Writing, as a means of communication, has its own unique power. Stating your intent in writing will strengthen your declaration.

The content of the declaration

Try to recall one or two examples of your child's extreme behaviour in the past. Present these examples to your child, to emphasize how intolerable is the situation in which your family now finds itself. Attempt, as far as possible, to include a descriptive, rather than judgmental, message in your declaration. For example, instead of saying, 'We will no longer suffer the terror you have wrought in our household,' say, 'We will no longer tolerate you beating up your brother and sister.'

Example of a draft declaration

Summary of situation

The violence in our household has become intolerable. (*Here should follow a list of concrete negative behaviours.*) We cannot, and do not wish to, live like this anymore. We intend to do all that we can to change this situation, though we will not attack you verbally or physically.

Plan of action

- We have decided to become more present in your life.

- We have decided not to face these problems alone any longer. We will seek out and turn to our friends and relatives, asking for their full involvement.

- We have decided to oppose resolutely the following behaviour. (*Here, cite one or two, but not more than three, specific examples of your child's extreme behaviour in the past.*)

- We do not want to overpower you, nor do we wish to defeat you.

- This statement bears no threat to you. It simply expresses our commitment to you, as your parents and as human beings.

The child's response to the declaration

The likelihood is that your child will resent the declaration. His reaction may be accompanied by direct escalation or by belittling, derisive words and actions. The child is following familiar response patterns, hoping to reap familiar reactions. You must meet these escalatory expressions with calm resolve. Responding quietly and choosing not to be drawn by your child's direct or implied invitation for escalation will be the initial example of the way you interact with your child from now on.

Should extreme behaviour reoccur following the declaration, you will need to recruit outside help in the form of friends and family who will bear witness to the child's bad behaviour and make the situation public – see Chapter 5, 'Telephone Rounds'.

We now move on from the declaration, or statement of intent, to action. We outline the tools employed in Non-Violent Resistance to achieve its goals.

Chapter 3

The Sit-In

One of the most potent activities parents can engage in when practising Non-Violent Resistance is the sit-in. The sit-in follows an extreme incident, allowing parents to demonstrate their presence while abstaining from confrontation and expressing resolve. Its purpose is to make it known to your child that you will no longer tolerate your child's aggression.

How does the sit-in work?

Choose a time that is convenient for you. Do not do this immediately after an extreme occurrence in the house, but at least a day later when you are calm and when you have blocked off a sufficient amount of time.

TIP: Do not execute the sit-in when you are stressed for time – you must not leave in the middle.

---

1. Enter your child's room when he is there, close the door to the room behind you and sit yourself down – on a chair, on the floor – in some way that makes it difficult for your child to leave the room.

2. Once sitting, tell your child calmly: 'We will no longer tolerate your behaviour. (*Proceed to describe the behaviour you object to, citing specific examples.*) We have come here to find a way to solve this problem. We would like to hear your suggestions.'

   • Parents who expect their child to become violent should invite an adult to the house (a friend or close family member) but not into the room with them. Following the opening words, tell your child: 'We have invited this person here today to be a witness because we are afraid that you may act violently.'

- Should the child become violent despite the presence of the witness, ask your guest to come into your child's room. Experience shows that the mere presence of a third party reduces the incidence of violence to near zero.

3. Sit quietly and await your child's suggestions.

4. Listen to what he has to say, and consider his words.

5. If they are accusations ('It is my brother's fault!'), demands ('Buy me a television set and I'll stop!'), or threats ('OK, I'm going to run away!'), do not take the bait. Avoid confrontation!

6. Tell your child what he says is unacceptable, and continue to sit quietly. Avoid blames, threats, sermons or arguments of any kind. Keep waiting quietly and patiently. Under no circumstances allow yourself to be led into a verbal or physical confrontation.

TIP: Time and silence project parental resolve.

---

7. Should your child make even the slightest positive suggestion, ask him to explain it.

8. Tell him positively that you will consider it and leave the room quietly. Do not threaten your child by saying that should he renege, you will come and sit in his room again. If the child repeats a

suggestion that he has made in the past, tell him: 'You have already made that suggestion and it did not help. We now need something that will work better.'

9. If the child has not made any suggestion, remain in his room for up to one hour, then walk out. Do not warn or threaten that you will return. When leaving, you could simply say: 'We have not yet found a solution.'

Key points to remember when conducting a sit-in

- The sit-in must be planned in advance by the parents.

- Undesirable behaviour must be clearly defined. Avoid using general messages, like 'We would like you to behave better.' Be specific: 'We want you to stop using foul language and to stop using hand gestures.'

- After the sit-in, continue with your daily household routine without referring to the sit-in or to its consequences.

Anticipating and preparing for your child's reaction

Your child will not like your entering his room and invading his space. There follows a series of scenarios that take into account possible reactions to the sit-in on the part of your child and the parental responses we recommend.

TIP: Remember it was you who engineered this sit-in and you have the power to set the rules.

Attempting to expel the parent

Your child may try expelling you from his room, for example by cursing or yelling 'Get out of here, I can't stand you!' This type of behaviour is best met with silence on your part. Do not be afraid that a reaction of silence from you would in any way mean that your dignity has been hurt.

Do not feel compelled to argue with your child. Being drawn into an argument would mean you have lost the initiative and were reacting to his provocation. The child may attempt to expel you through physical violence – throwing things or pushing you out of the door. When this occurs, defend yourself but do not attack your child. If you anticipate violence, make sure to invite a guest to the sit-in. Should your child begin acting in a violent way that can only be checked by your own display of force, stop the sit-in and leave his room. You can begin again, any time you desire, and in the presence of witnesses. It is very important that you remain able to stop any action deemed highly escalatory. Here, you are required to use your common sense.

TIP: Remember, retreating to regroup is not the same as giving up.

Imposing terms on the parents

The child may attempt to stop the sit-in by imposing terms such as 'I'll do what you want if you buy me this or that.' Should this happen, say you cannot accept his offer, then go back to being silent again and await his further reaction.

Ignoring the parents

In ignoring you, your child is sending you the message that your actions have had no effect on him. He may turn on the television, stereo, or start up his computer. When this happens turn off the appliances, but do it only once. If the child decides to turn it back on, avoid further attempts and continue to sit until the sit-in is over.

Another type of reaction, meant to demonstrate ignorance of your presence, is lying in bed pretending to be asleep. Time passes very slowly when the child pretends to be sleeping! Even if he has indeed fallen asleep, continue the sit-in without interruption. The child falling asleep while you're in his room signifies a change in attitude which can be taken to mean: 'I accept you staying in my room and offer you some measure of trust.' This is in contrast to anything the child might have said when awake.

Trying to embarrass and humiliate the parents by shouting loudly

In doing this, the child is trying to use the neighbours or other outside parties to interfere and stop the sit-in. If you expect this type of behaviour and are afraid of its repercussions, you may want to take the precaution of informing your neighbours beforehand about what is about to happen as well as the reasons for your planned actions.

Trying to provoke the parents into speaking

The child may attempt to lead you back to your old familiar role, where you continue to speak and he refuses to relate to what you are saying. He may do this by repeating, for example: 'I don't understand what you want of me!' Or, he may attempt to draw you into an argument. It is best not to respond but to maintain your silence. Any attempt to explain beyond your brief opening statement is counter-productive.

Accepting a positive offer made by the child

When your child makes a positive offer or suggestion, ask him about his offer, but only if it is concrete. An offer like 'I'll be a good boy!' requires clarification. When the child has come up with even a slight but realistic offer, end the sit-in and walk out of the room. Do not be afraid that the child has played you for a fool – if his behaviour does not improve you can always return to continue the sit-in.

When to initiate further sit-ins

The purpose of the sit-in is to reduce the occurrence of problematic behaviour in the future. The purpose of the sit-in is *not* that your child behaves during the sit-in itself. Even if your child swears and curses at you throughout the sit-in, it does not mean that your action has been in vain.

It is important to realize that often children change their problematic behaviour without having made any offer during the sit-in. The sit-in is planned to affect both your child's behaviour and your own position in the family. Such effects occur whether your child has or has not made an offer. Should your child attempt to hold on to his dignity by refusing to make an offer, yet change his behaviour for the better, accept this as progress. The sit-in doesn't only change your child, it changes you as well. You discover that you are able to walk into your child's room and stay sitting there for as long as you have planned. You no longer let yourself be expelled, and you can avoid escalation. Most important, you learn that you carry personal and parental weight. Your place in the family has changed immeasurably.

What determines the need for further sit-ins is the intensity of your child's problematic behaviours following the sit-in. Should you sense a diminishing of the problems, no further sit-ins will be needed. If on the other hand, you feel that problems are continuing, you must initiate further sit-ins.

TIP: Repeat to yourself when faced with adversity: 'Abstain, never yield.'

Chapter 4

Going Public

Recruiting the help of others

One of the most important ingredients for the success of your plan to resist your child's violent or destructive behaviour is to share the situation with others. Families who are suffering from continuing violent situations are often characterized by a shroud of secrecy hovering over the home. Experience shows that secrecy often feeds violence. It is a natural reaction to want to keep things quiet in order to protect yourselves and your children. Yet foregoing all avenues of help and support in the desire to avoid being stigmatized, can create isolation and compound the cycle of violence.

Recruiting outside help and making the situation transparent is not an easy decision to make. You must overcome your inhibitions in carrying it through. However, once you have crossed that hurdle, and you have gathered sufficient inner strength to proceed, you will be fortified by the support of the people around you, and you will find that your child responds positively to your newfound support. Your self-confidence will increase as a result, as will your trust in the path that you have chosen. In many instances, the mere knowledge that you are not alone itself suffices in discernibly diminishing your child's extreme behaviour.

You must draw a number of people into your confidence, including both friends and family members. Stop viewing your child's difficult behaviour as a close-kept secret. Make your child aware that the veil of silence has been lifted; his behaviour is now transparent and, therefore, as a family and a parental authority you are no longer alone. From now on things will be called what they are – 'violence' or 'exploitation'.

TIP: Remember that breaking the circle of silence and drawing on outside support hastens an end to the cycle of violence.

Introducing transparency to the child

Ask those you have informed of the situation to contact the child personally or by telephone, mail or email to tell your child that they have been fully informed of his behaviour. Contact from far-away friends or relatives, whom the child holds in high regard, is especially effective.

- Ask your friends and family to refer specifically to the latest occurrence and to make it clear to the child that they regard such behaviour as completely unacceptable.

- If your child has been violent towards you or towards other family members, or has destroyed property, they must let him know that this type of behaviour constitutes 'violence within the family' and is considered a violation of the law.

- In general, your friends and family must impart to your child their resolve to help you stop the situation, and their intention to fully support you.

The purpose of communication between your supporters and your child is to clarify to your child that he can no longer hide his deeds, that his behaviour is catching outside attention, and that those who know about it stand firmly behind you, but intend to support him too.

TIP: It is advisable that you suggest friends and family members read this guidebook too, so that they can familiarize themselves with the strategies and principles associated with the Non-Violent Resistance Approach.

The value of mediation

Inviting outsiders to become involved may open up new avenues towards solutions. Beyond supporting you and serving as channels of moral persuasion (by representing public opinion), your supporters may potentially act as mediators. Among your friends or family members, you may find a person who is capable of communicating with the child, possibly working out compromises with him.

Why use a mediator?

- Both parties – you and your child – are suffering from a lack of communication.

- The child feels that he must hold on to his position to maintain his dignity.

It is in times of crisis that mediators are most effective. A mediator may help persuade your child to back off from extreme positions in situations where your appeals would be automatically rejected (for example, he or she might be able to persuade a child to come out of his room or return home). A mediator can also be very helpful when linking (see Chapter 6, 'Linking'). A mediator greatly helps to minimize the loneliness children often feel under the new set of circumstances, so by simply involving this third person, you have acted to reduce escalation and polarization.

Chapter 5

Telephone Rounds

Having made the situation public, you are now in a position to instigate telephone rounds when necessary. Possible responses your child may have to the conflict or to your attempts to change the status quo include not bothering to tell you where he is going, or disappearing for hours at a time, overnight or for even longer. In order to communicate your parental presence effectively, you must pursue contact with your child even when he is away from home. Telephone rounds involve you calling every person your child keeps, or has kept, in touch with, in the event that he runs away or you don't know where he is.

The main purpose of doing the telephone rounds is not to bring the child back home. First and foremost, it is important for you to reassume the position of supervisor, and you must fully restore your presence as a parent. Telephone rounds achieve all that even when you have not located your child! By making the telephone calls you leave your mark in many areas of your child's life. With each telephone call you expand your presence. You have passed on a message to him that you object to his disappearance, and that you have expanded your network of support.

The aims of telephone rounds

- To restore both your parental presence and supervision of your child without resorting to violence.

- To demonstrate your disapproval of your child's disappearances and of his participation in certain activities, and your willingness to challenge these behaviours.

- To locate the child.

- To apply peer pressure to convince the child to come back home.

Telephone rounds reinforce the 'transparency' principle. Not only have you caused the child to return, you have proven that you are adamant about reaching out for help and about never again being alone to deal with your problems. This is a central tenet of the Non-Violent Resistance Model. In contacting others to show your parental concern, you promulgate the cause of your struggle. Therefore don't be surprised to find that you have won the support of parents who find themselves in similar circumstance to your own. The practical steps to take in making telephone rounds are explained below.

Step 1: Collecting numbers

Start by collecting the telephone numbers of your child's friends and acquaintances. Include other children, coaches, youth guides, club managers as well as the

places you think that your child may be when away from home – the sports club, video arcade, pub or disco, for example. Gathering those numbers may be done using all available means and networking. For instance, you may ask a friend of your child, whose telephone number you already have, to give you telephone numbers of other friends that you do not have.

Step 2: Calling contacts

Implement the next step either when your child is inexplicably late coming home, when he runs away or when he has disappeared. Should this occur you must call all the people and places on your prepared list. Be sure to call every number on your list, not only the places where you think you may find him. It is also important to continue your telephone rounds even after your child has been found – *each number must be contacted.* It is important to note that although you want to find your child, you also want to pass him the important message that you, his parents, are present wherever he may be.

TIP: Calling your child on his mobile phone will not address the issue, as your child can turn off this phone as a way of disappearing.

Speaking with your child's friends

Introduce yourself. Say that your child has disappeared and that you have been looking for him. Ask the friend to tell you if he has seen your child at school that day, if he has heard of your child's plans, or if he has any idea where your child may be. Ask him to convey your concern to your child and to tell your child that you have been looking for him. Ask him if he could in any way convince your child to contact you.

This is a crucial moment in the conversation. According to his response, you will know if you have found someone who can act the part of mediator. If he is open to the possibility of offering you some assistance, try setting up a meeting between yourself and this friend. Expanding your network of support to include some of your child's friends is an important achievement. This expansion may prove critical. When you finish speaking with him, ask to speak with one of his parents.

Speaking with your child's friends' parents

Introduce yourself in the same way. Ask if the friends' parents have seen your child lately. Also ask them not to let your child sleep over without your prior explicit consent. Often you will find willing allies in these parents, especially if they suffer similar problems. Try to meet with them. There is great potential in these parents' networks.

Speaking with the owners and employees of hangout spots

Often, employees will know the child personally through regular contact, and thus they can be an especially useful ally. On the one hand, they are used to working with young people. On the other hand, they are capable of understanding the concern of a parent. Ask these people to try to locate your child on the spot, or at least give him a message that you are looking for him.

Remember: Even if they don't know your child, the most important point is that you went there, you spoke to them, you left a message – you were there and you were present. There is no longer a taboo about whom you speak to and where you go to demonstrate your deep concern for your child. Ultimately, this concern will resonate not only with those associated with your child but, most importantly, with your child himself. In spite of everything, he will remember that 'My parents were here. My parents were looking for me. My parents care about me.'

Step 3: Completing the rounds

Proceed to call every number even if you have located your child or if he has returned home. If it is too late to make telephone rounds, wait until the next day. Be sure to tell everyone that your child was missing the previous night and that you were terribly worried. Ask them to tell you all they know, and ask if they would be willing to help in the future. Should he disappear again, would they help you to trace your child or otherwise convince him to get in touch with you? If your child later protests that you needlessly embarrassed him (he is home after all), tell him calmly that you have decided that you will no longer accept his disappearances. Apply to these telephone rounds the same rules which have been emphasized until now.

1. Categorically avoid verbally expressing any negative or aggressive thoughts about your child or his behaviour.

2. Refer to your child respectfully and avoid saying anything that may humiliate him.

3. Do not use guilt or accusations to appeal to your network.

4. Try to gain their sympathy and support.

You will probably have located your child through telephone rounds. Another powerful tool you may choose to use is linking, which is described in more detail in the next chapter.

Chapter 6

Linking

The parental action of 'linking' is designed to minimize 'dead spaces' (i.e. unsupervised spaces) created by disappearances, unreported and unauthorized absences, and by the child's other hidden activities. Linking takes place when parents search for their child and insist on appearing in those places deemed taboo for adults – places that may be dangerous including disco clubs, abandoned beaches or parks.

Research has shown that children who can no longer be controlled detach themselves from their parents – and that this may lead to deviation and to extreme and unusual behaviour by the child. (Any behaviour that is age or developmentally inappropriate, or socially or legally inappropriate, is defined as deviant.) This detachment tends to be the result of some previous escalation, and in turn leads to further escalations. The purpose of linking, therefore, is not only to prevent problematic developments caused by questionable unsupervised activities, but also to prevent the escalations caused by detachment itself. In other words, instead of reacting to the child's withdrawal by detaching yourself from your child – for instance by locking him out, or by angrily deciding to 'let the kid do what he wants!', or by instigating further escalation through the use of punishment and counter-punishment – you link. Linking enhances parental presence, acting to obstruct the process of detachment and deterring further escalation.

When to link

It is recommended that you link to your child under the following circumstances:

- *When the child runs away from home:* Children often seek shelter with friends, extended family members, runaway shelters and among fringe groups defined as alternative youth cultures. Remember that although running away is regarded as an extreme reaction on the child's part, he continues to expect you, his parents, to come looking for him.

- *When the child misses curfew or disappears for long hours during the day*: In contrast to running away from home which may be considered an exceptional event indicating substantial family or individual turbulence, missing curfew and daily disappearances may come to be regarded as more routine occurrences. The child thus sees them as 'basic rights' long awarded him by his parents. As a result the child may show greater surprise and resistance at seeing his parents appear in his hangouts, than he might after running away from home.

- *When the child spends time in questionable company with other people who may be contributing toward his behaviour*: It is generally believed that keeping bad company foretells one's decline. Left unsupervised, your child may begin engaging in substance abuse, skipping school or taking part in delinquent and dangerous activities.

Rules to follow when linking

- Announce that you want your child back home and that he need not fear repercussions.

- Avoid all arguments and whenever possible try to keep quiet.

- Avoid all physical actions that might lead to escalation – for example, grabbing your child and forcing him into your car.

- Arrive at places frequented by your child and spend as much time as you can near him.

TIP: Remember that the success of your linking is measured not by your ability to bring your child back, but by the power of your parental presence in resisting his detachment.

Warning

As with the other Non-Violent Resistance tools (sit-ins, telephone rounds, implementing the transparency principle, winning public opinion) linking will also cause your child to react in ways calculated to thwart your parental action and to re-establish the old order of things by:

- attempting to create confrontation

- attempting to further detach by running away or by shutting himself in.

To counter these reactions, you must carefully adhere to the principle of 'not being drawn in' (see Chapter 1) and continue to resolutely maintain your supervision and contact with the child.

Linking scenarios

How best to form a link may vary with the situation. Some examples follow.

Linking while the child is at a friend's house

Ring the doorbell and say you have come to take your child home. If he comes forward, reassure him that you have no intention of punishing him but that you insist he come home with you. If he tries to evade you, say you are waiting for him. Ask his friend, or his friend's parents, to let you wait inside the house. If you are not invited in, remain where you are and continue ringing the doorbell every ten minutes or so, asking that your child come home with you.

Linking when the child is hanging out on the street or at a club

Approach your child and let him know that you expect him to come home with you and that you will not punish him. If he runs away – a typical reaction – do not chase after him. Instead, use the time to get to know his friends. Introduce yourself, ask them their names and for their telephone numbers and tell them about your difficult situation. Do not assume that they will oppose you; some may sympathize with your actions. During the conversation you might say: 'My child may be different from you. He may be putting himself in danger more often, as some of you may have more self-control than he does.' Or if your child's friends are older than he is, if he is considered a rookie, you might say, 'You may already enjoy a greater degree of freedom. My kid is only 14!' or 'You may know when you've had enough, when it's time to quit drinking, for instance. But I'm afraid, and maybe you have noticed yourself, that my child has little control over such things.'

Talking in this way may serve to build alliances, helping you find support where you least expected to find it. Some of these children may, in the future, play the crucial role of mediators. In our experience, friends recruited in this way have often brought back a runaway child.

Linking when your child has run away

When your child has run away to join others his age who are living together for an unspecified period of time (in a commune, for instance), follow the previous guidance, remembering that this time linking may take longer. In one case we know of, for example, the parents sat on the beach where the young people lived for three days before their daughter, who had been missing from home for over a month, consented to come home with them.

Having a friend or family member join you while linking can be helpful in all the situations described above. It is good to have backup when visiting frightening locations where you think you may find your child – for example, when the child may be mingling in the company of drug dealers or users.

The impact of linking may be greater when you are accompanied. Your companion may be able to bridge the gap between you and your child, helping you find a suitable compromise, thus allowing your child to 'save face'.

TIP: Never try to overpower your child, as this will result in escalation. By simply going and staying, you are demonstrating parental presence.

Chapter 7

The Sit-Down Strike

A sit-down strike, in its make-up and content, may be described as a rite of passage. Rites of passage are meant to signal to individuals, family, and the community that life is at a crossroads. That is to say that the situation known before the ritual will markedly differ from the situation following the ritual. The ritual itself is a symbolic event. Even more, it brings about new conditions that promote change in the behaviour of child and parent alike.

A sit-down strike involves staying at home for three days with the child, the rest of the family and as many supporters as possible, in an attempt to find a way out of the situation that does not involve punishment.

Aims of a sit-down strike

- To respond appropriately to sharp escalations from your child, such as running away from home or striking a parent.
- To recruit and demonstrate support for the parents and family.
- To demonstrate parental presence powerfully.

Preparing for a sit-down strike

Blocking off time

You must clear at least three full calendar days; it is possible to add one weekday to the weekend to make up these three days.

Inviting guests

A central condition for the successful execution of a sit-down strike is maximum publicity. The extreme events preceding the strike justify breaking the bounds of discretion. Breaking silence constitutes a radical change in future family life, thus anointing the strike as a true rite of passage.

Try to contact as many friends, relatives and other people close to your child – teachers, youth guides, his friends and their parents – as possible. Describe your plans and the reasons behind them. You might say: 'We ask for your help in the wake of recent developments (*detail recent events*). Following this event, we have decided to hold a three-day sit-down strike at our home. We are asking friends, family, and people who are close to our child to come visit, to help us in trying to come up with a solution. We will be home with our child for all three days. Your presence is very important to us all.'

Should invitees make comments doubting the need for the strike, say: 'We are doing this because we are afraid of losing our child. We are seeking counsel and asking for help before it is too late.' Through their participation, guests become witnesses to and supporters of the parents' declaration that the situation cannot go on and requires immediate change. Some of the guests may take part in drafting a proposal or in executing practical or temporary solutions. They may lend a hand in helping the child with his studies, taking him out for exercise or, at a later time, having him over for the weekend or for a short vacation.

Preparing food and types of involvement

Bringing food is a primary, fundamental expression of support. It is recommended that you ask friends and family if they can bring food with them or cook for you while they visit. Those who cannot be present are asked at least to call and speak with the parents and to ask to speak with the child. Friends and family abroad may take part, using the telephone, fax or email.

Preparing your home

Home preparations include:

- taking the keys to your child's bedroom so that he cannot lock himself in during the strike

- preparing food to last three days or asking close friends or relatives to bring food with them

- making yourself available to watch your child.

Initiating the strike

The sit-down strike begins when the child is at home and a small group of supporters is present (two to three people). It is recommended that you invite a friend of your child over too – one who has agreed to help you and your child find a way out of your present entanglement. The presence of one of his friends helps diminish polarization, which could occur if only your friends are present. Your announcement marks the opening of the event, and could be worded something like this:

> We have decided to hold a three-day sit-down strike in order to reach a solution to recent event X (*describe the event*). During these three days we will all stay at home. People who wish to help us will visit. We will not work, nor entertain ourselves, nor will we leave this house. (*Your child's name*) will remain with us. We will not chastise you or punish you. Whatever solution we reach, it will not include punishing you, for that is not our purpose. We simply want our family to find its way out of this situation.

If you cannot impart this message directly to your child, ask a mediator to convey the message to him.

What happens if your child tries to leave the house?

You should try to stop your child from leaving the house, even if it means locking the house door. Should the child leave the house anyway, continue the strike as planned while conducting a wide circle of telephone rounds. Once you have located your child, start linking with the help of your supporters. Insofar as it is possible, one parent should continue the strike at home while the other links. In single parent households, one guest should remain at home to play host to the visitors. Should your child refuse to speak with you or with your guests, continue the strike as planned, asking your guests to greet your child upon entering and to write him a farewell note before leaving. Do not try to force your child to communicate under any circumstances.

TIP: Encourage guests to bring small gifts or symbolic items to give the child as they leave – such as a greeting card, a flower, or a favourite food or treat. These can represent gestures of reconciliation from the 'outside world'.

What happens if your child hurls accusations and tries to humiliate you?

Should the child vociferously accuse you of aggression, compulsion, humiliation or treachery, you must reply in person or via mediators:

> 'We have no intention of punishing or humiliating you, nor have we any intention of overpowering you. As your parents and protectors, it is our duty to do everything we can to change and heal our relationship with you. The situation in our home has got so out of hand that it has forced us to take these special measures.'

TIP: Parents are advised not to shy away from ceremonious language, as this act is a ceremony, a rite of passage. Nevertheless, you must express yourself in appropriate terms that a child will understand.

On this, guests must stand by the parents, helping them convey their message concisely. If your child is willing to communicate with a small group of people or even with just one person, they/he/she must become the mediator or mediators. The mediator's role is to bridge the gap between parent and child while avoiding the assignment of blame to either party. The mediator must also have come to the conclusion that 'the present situation is intolerable and must not be allowed to continue'. The mediator's suggestions will be discussed by the parents and put to the consideration of guests who are present or friends who can be reached by phone.

How do you end the sit-down strike?

By no means should the strike end with threats or sanctions. It is best to conclude it in writing, by thanking those who have come for their friendship and support. Convey your thoughts in writing to everyone, including your child. These thoughts should not take the form of an agreement that your child signs. Rather, there must be a written account which briefly describes the whole rite of passage.

Ask your guests to continue calling the family and the child in the weeks following the strike. After a big event like a sit-down strike, you might think that in the future, your responses to your child's difficult behaviour must be on the same grandiose level. This is not the case. Your response to his behaviour should remain within the normal measures of Non-Violent Resistance (sit-ins, telephone rounds, the Non-Violent Resistance Model, and reconciliation). However, the strike has now created a new reality, which allows the parent to operate within the supporting reach of friends and extended family.

Chapter 8

Refusing Orders

While sit-ins, telephone rounds and sit-down strikes are effective responses to extreme events, refusing orders is something you can incorporate into everyday routine. Your child has probably become used to being chauffeured, to being served upon demand, to his food being prepared just the way he likes it, to the television being turned to his favourite shows and so forth. The purpose of refusing orders is to shake the foundations of the unbalanced, intolerable reality taken as an absolute given by your child.

We may feel that over the years some gradual unfelt process has turned us from parents who can say 'no' to some of our child's demands, into parents completely obedient to our child's every whim. Through this process, our freedom of action has been dramatically narrowed, while our child's freedom to display his disruptive behaviour has continued to grow. As we have been 'trained' to follow his will, so he has grown less sensitive to ours. Eventually, we may have come to regard ourselves as slaves to his wants and unable to 'disobey' him.

The purpose of refusing orders is to liberate us from feeling abused and oppressed by our child. By refusing orders we discover that this abnormal situation cannot exist without our consent. We will also discover that we never truly consented, but have given away our rights of consent under the implicit or explicit threat of being punished by our child.

Refusing orders is a stage in Non-Violence Resistance where, as parents:

1. We refuse to carry out actions which we have felt compelled to perform in the past, for example, giving out spending money, chauffeuring, and so on.

2. We reinstate important activities which we have been prevented from carrying out in the past, for example, entering the child's room, checking or putting his belongings in order when necessary.

As parents we thus signal our termination of any obedience patterns which have developed over time, patterns which perpetuate escalation.

Aims of refusing orders

- To terminate parental yielding patterns.

- To make parents aware of the services we provide and challenge the child not to take these services for granted.

- To provide us as parents with a wider range of possibilities for reaching our child.

TIP: Think of refusing orders as an attempt to break your patterns of obedience, and thus uncover your own will and voice as parents. It is not a way to punish your child.

Methods of being disobedient

Refusing orders takes place on two complementary dimensions:

- *Service strike*: This is where you stop all services given to your child under explicit or implicit duress.

- *Breaking taboo*: This is when you conduct parental activities which have until now been forbidden by your child.

Service strike

In order to prepare, you must assess and re-evaluate all the services you provide to your child. Try to distinguish between services provided willingly and unnecessary services provided under duress. Services provided under your child's coercion are frequently associated with the demand implicitly or explicitly expressed: 'Do this or I will...' followed by a threat of some kind.

As parents you then need to choose which of those imposed services to stop. Some examples of services which parents choose to include in their strikes are: driving the child to classes, friends' houses or parties, providing luxury foods or drinks, answering demands for particular dishes, providing metered services such as mobile phones which the child uses indiscriminately, or responding to any command deemed unreasonable to you. The stronger the child's demands for a particular service, the more likely that it was given unwillingly.

TIP: The more loudly the child demands the service, the more likely that it fits the category of services that should be put on strike!

The conduct and aims of this strike differ radically from the conduct and aims of punishments:

- The reason a service is put on strike is not that the child has behaved badly. Rather, it is the parents' realization that such service is not given of their free will but given by them under the child's implied or actual coercion.

- Services will not be restored once the child behaves well. (Parents may restore certain services if they wish once they are convinced that the threat attached to the service and their reaction to the threat has been removed.)

- While punishment is meant to alter the child's behaviour, the strike seeks to improve parents' self-confidence and terminate any patterns of obedience, putting an end to their feelings of being used. The strike may very well contribute to improving the child's behaviour but that achievement stands secondary to the change sought in the parents' self-worth and in their enhanced parental presence.

TIP: Remember that the service strike is not a punishment.

Breaking taboo

In preparing for breaking taboo, you must identify areas of your life at home where free access and peoples' freedom of movement have been severely limited by your child. Such common taboos are: restricted access to your child's room, restrictions on inviting guests (either who you invite or when you invite them), inability to arrange your home according to your taste, restricted television viewing in the living room, limited telephone access and more.

Perhaps your friends and family have in the past directed your attention to your over-accommodating acceptance of certain restrictions from your child. Those areas of parental obedience are perfect for breaking taboo. When you have decided which 'taboo' to break, inform those who have previously identified this problem and other potential supporters of your decision.

Anticipating your child's reaction

Expect that in this area too your child will try to break your resistance using threats, violence or accusations. According to previously taught principles, your response must be: abstain and do not yield! Moreover, you may choose to respond by employing various Non-Violent Resistance tools. For instance, in response to violence you may initiate a sit-in to mobilize public support. In response to running away, you may initiate telephone rounds and so on.

Telling your child in advance of your refusal to carry out orders

Inform your child that you intend to refuse to carry out his orders, in a discreet and calm manner. Take care to steer away from an 'I am the boss!' stance which your child could see as threatening. Simply tell your child calmly, 'I will no longer do X.' Do not explain yourself, do not try to justify or argue – all of that will ultimately lead to escalation.

Result

By means of refusing orders and breaking taboo you have stopped automatically obeying your child and have regained your decision-making power. That sense of freedom felt immediately upon establishing boundaries regarding your child's demands, will help empower you in your continuing struggle to overcome the extreme and disruptive behaviour of your child. As forearmed parents, who no longer obey our children's every whim, we are able to change not only the atmosphere at home, but also our own sense of self. Refusing orders leads to a substantial re-evaluation of our self-worth.

At the end of this process, you will be able to reinstate some of the services which you terminated, perhaps driving your child places from time to time, letting him have his own mobile phone within clear limits and so on. Reinstatement, however, depends not only upon your child's behaviour but principally upon your decree. You must ask yourself: 'Am I sure that there are no threats attached? Do I really want to reinstate this service? Will I feel free to withhold the service if the circumstances change?' Such questioning takes into account our views and wishes alone, not those of the child. Termination and/or reinstatement of services depends upon us alone.

Chapter 9

Reconciliation

In order that conflicts and power struggles do not become the axis around which your relationship with your child revolves, it is vital to perform 'acts of reconciliation'. Research into escalation shows that reconciliatory acts greatly diminish escalatory threats. Reconciliatory acts minimize resentment at home, helping to build a broader, more positively based relationship. Reconciliatory acts should not be conditional upon the actions and behaviour of your child. They are not to be taken as rewards, nor should the child be punished by their withdrawal. Through giving, acts of reconciliation enable us to become loving parents again, while simultaneously continuing our unyielding struggle of Non-Violent Resistance.

Avenues of reconciliation

Words: Verbal or written

Say and write things that are respectful of your child, his talents, his attributes and his world view. Show him that you appreciate and respect that he pursues what is important to him.

Treats: Preparing his favourite meal or buying his favourite foods

When presenting your child with a favourite meal, do not insist that he accepts what you have prepared. If you have cooked his favourite meal, do not be adamant that he eats it right away and that he eats it with you. Treats are unconditional gestures of giving, from you to your child. Your child will choose his own way to accept or refuse them. Avoid giving expensive items or services. Certainly do not give anything that the child demands as a pre-condition to improving his behaviour, recalling the principles in the previous chapter.

Mending

A meaningful gesture may be to fix the child's favourite toy or a favourite household item that he broke during a fit of anger. Repairing an object symbolizes repairing the relationship. Do not be afraid of being perceived as weak.

> **TIP:** You do not want to be seen as all powerful, in overcoming your child. You want to be seen as caring parents.

Suggesting positive family activities

Suggest activities you can do together, for example, walking, going to a movie, engaging in sports or exercise, or participating in some other regular activity your child enjoys.

> **TIP:** If your child refuses, do not think of this as 'losing points'.

Expressing remorse

A very special reconciliatory act is expressing regret over some past parental act of aggression. Parents tend to shy away from expressing their regret, for fear of being considered weak.

How will your child respond to your acts of reconciliation?

Your child is unlikely to interpret your acts of reconciliation as signs of weakness. Most likely, he will accept them for what they truly are: voluntary attempts at reconciliation. Acts of reconciliation express your heartfelt desire to expand your relationship with your child beyond the narrow confines of difficult encounters and power struggles.

However, it is probable that your child will, at first, reject your attempts at reconciliation. Remember that rejection does not mean you have failed in your initiative. Your child is simply trained by habit to arbitrarily reject all your advances. In spite of his rejection, your actions are truly worthwhile as they help to consolidate and project your positive presence as parents in your child's life. Do not relent in your attempts to reconcile with your child – even when he rejects you.

TIP: Never force your child to accept your gestures. Just keep trying.

Chapter 10

Summary: Empowerment and Readiness

The means and tools of Non-Violent Resistance that we have described are designed to empower you. The various techniques presented were not randomly assembled. Non-Violent Resistance is not achieved by simply holding a sit-in or by picking up the phone to do telephone rounds. The process becomes powerful only when the tools and the principles are combined.

To recap, the actions at your disposal, as we have seen, are:

- *declaring* that you no longer accept the present situation

- *breaking silence* and gathering support

- *asking supporters* to let the child know that they have been informed of his behaviour

- *sit-ins*

- *telephone rounds*

- *linking*

- *finding allies* among your child's friends and their parents

- *sit-down strikes*

- *refusing orders* by ending all extorted services and breaking taboo

- *acts of reconciliation*

- *never yielding*

- *not being drawn in* to potentially escalatory behaviour.

One action reinforces the next. Focusing on the task at hand, we prove to ourselves and to our child that life at home has radically changed. Preparing ourselves for this task requires resolve, a strong sense of responsibility and moral fortitude. In order to guarantee success, we must assign top priority to Non-Violent Resistance. Our experience has shown that as parents we need three months of full focus on the methods and principles described to have a lasting impact on our child's behaviour.

Once this period is over, the situation will have irreversibly changed. You will discover that being alert and attentive to the Non-Violent Resistance approach requires less and less effort on your part, because you have developed new habits which are now established. What may have characterized you in the past – for example, yielding and being unable to abstain from emotional involvement and escalatory patterns – gradually becomes foreign and irrelevant. When your child tries to provoke you, he does not elicit your old ingrained reactions. The new situation brings with it a deep-felt change in your home and in your relationship with your child.

In order to reach this stage in the process, we must resist the urge to achieve immediate results. Parents who expect change after just one or two sit-ins will inevitably be disappointed.

TIP: You need to become fully enlisted by investing a significant amount of time in being a practical, focused parental presence. You need to spend time sitting-in, making telephone rounds, building support, linking and so on in order to see a significant improvement in your child's behaviour.

Once the initial effort has been made, you will notice your child's first signs of accommodation. At times you may doubt just how much the situation with your child has changed. These doubts can be useful and are certainly justified. They stop us from becoming complacent. Do not assume that your child has already responded to the approach, that he has found a new path. Deep-felt changes are happening within you! You are learning to respond differently, think differently, and slowly starting to feel differently. As these changes take root within you, your child's potential for risky, destructive behaviour will inevitably, decrease eventually, but it will take time.

You need to develop resilience, and steel yourself for your child's tough to deal with reactions. You cannot expect a child accustomed to what he perceives as power and independence, to simply give it all away. Your child will do everything to convince you that your efforts are fruitless, that you have no chance of success, and that by acting as you do you are only making things worse. Your child will want you to surrender and be drawn into conflict again and again.

If in the past your child was capable of derailing you – of making you surrender, of involving you in conflict by arguing, by throwing insults or curses, by threatening, by playing the victim, by worrying you or inducing guilt in you – he will inevitably try it again!

TIP: Be especially vigilant and aware of the dangers of being drawn into violent outbursts, verbal or physical. Each violent outburst can take days to heal.

Guard yourself against any aggressive reactions by remembering and then implementing the following principles:

- *Expect and prepare for your child's hard-hitting reactions.* Your position is much stronger if you are not caught by surprise. If you're prepared, while events may still be difficult, they are at least tolerable.

- *Remember that extreme reactions are short-lived.* Your child will not continue escalating his response forever. The more extreme his reaction, the shorter it will last. When you do not yield, when you continue to refrain from being drawn into conflict, your child's harsh reactions will lose their hold. Without your expected reaction, his own reactions are denied the 'fuel' required for escalation.

- *Call upon your supporters* to help you absorb and withstand your child's difficult reactions. Aside from the obvious support they provide, recruiting friends and family members to help you can reinforce the message that you are resolving to maintain your new course.

- *Employ mediators to mitigate crises.* Among your supporting friends and family, find mediators who are able to communicate with your child. This special contact will help to ease your child's sense of loneliness, and may help to preserve his dignity in addition to moderating his responses.

Key message

Remember, above all, that yielding to your child's behaviour guarantees subsequent escalation. By contrast, calmly maintaining your presence as parents and adhering to the principles of the Non-Violent Resistance Model, protects your relationship with your child. It shields him from the disruptive effects of his own behaviour and enables you to best protect him from harm. Ultimately, the Non-Violent Resistance Model serves to empower you fully to resume your natural role as a parent and allows your child to revert to his natural role as your child.

Non-Violent Resistance in Practice

Thomas in the beginning

Any attempts to rein in Thomas's bouts of aggression were counteracted by a violent response, sometimes resulting in Thomas banging his head against a wall shouting 'I don't want to live anymore', 'I deserve to die', 'I am a bad boy', 'I deserve punishment' or even 'hit me'. This pattern of behaviour was also repeated at kindergarten and at home, causing his parents and teachers to feel they were in a state of 'total paralysis'.

The parents swung between no response at all and an aggressive response that included shouting at Thomas, shaking him, pushing and slapping him in the face. Thomas is not only the 'terror of the kindergarten' but also the 'horror of the home', deepening the social isolation that his family finds itself in, and eventually causing them to avoid being seen in public with him altogether. His parents felt ashamed that their child's behaviour was so obvious in public. Thomas's dad detached himself from the situation and the family began to be seen as outsiders. Everyone felt weak and helpless. They became cautious, with the attitude 'whatever you do, don't set him off'.

Using the Non-Violent Resistance approach

To help Thomas, it was necessary to form a plan. The initial aims were to help his parents:

- to see that the behaviour in the kindergarten and at home were the result of the same underlying problem

- to break out of their disengagement and re-assert themselves as central figures in Thomas's life

- to support each other and improve their relationships with neighbours and friends.

The first session – looking for clues

The first step was to identify those situations that were likely to result in escalation. Both parents brought up examples of situations where they found it difficult to convey a clear message to Thomas without either falling into the trap of wordy and lengthy discussions (Dad) or military style commands (Mum). Dad's difficulty was that he believed that Thomas would interpret an unambiguous style of interaction as authoritarian commands. He recounted his own traumatic experience of an authoritarian father that he still carries with him, stating that in the little time that he has to spend with his kids, he does not wish to exercise his power over them and command them.

NON-VIOLENT RESISTANCE TECHNIQUES

- *Tone of voice:* Mum is encouraged to avoid preaching, cajoling or threatening exchanges. Both parents are encouraged to use a quiet tone of voice and express a clear message.

- *Sleeping and waking up routines:* Thomas will wake up half an hour earlier than usual. This time will be used to pamper him.

- *Keeping Thomas in mind:* On the mornings when Dad is responsible for taking him to kindergarten, Mum will phone Thomas before he leaves the house and wish him a pleasant journey to kindergarten with his dad. Dad is expected to do likewise on days when Mum takes Thomas to kindergarten.

- *Leisure time:* On Thomas's return from kindergarten there are specific times allocated for watching TV and playing with the computer; such activities invariably became a focus of arguments in the past. The routine is expected to leave time for 'fun and leisure' – pampering, joking, and playing – activities that require full concentration and emotional attention from Mum.

Both parents agree to read this book so that they can understand the ideas in the approach fully.

The second session – understanding why

The talk returned to how the parents and the kindergarten team interacted with Thomas when confronted with his self-destructive and suicidal expressions. The parents and the team interpreted Thomas's self-destructive talk as a desperate attempt to test the parents' and kindergarten team's presence and their determination to stay the course with him.

NON-VIOLENT RESISTANCE TECHNIQUES

- *Addressing the child's self-esteem*: Everyone emphasizes a forceful resistance to Thomas's self-destructive ideas saying, 'We do not accept your hard opinion of yourself!'

- *Increasing the child's sense of security*: The parents will stress their commitment to love and protect Thomas, to refrain from insulting or shouting at him. They will apologize for all the hurts they may have caused him in the past and underline their determination that at their home there will be no more shouting and physical violence.

- *Respecting each other's personal space*: Any hugging and kissing will from now on be done only with Thomas's and his parents' explicit and mutual permission.

Parents are advised to be respectful in the way that they express intimate, physical attachment to their child.

The natural way to demonstrate love is through physical affection. Normally, we do not ask permission to hug or kiss; it is spontaneous. However, when we are trying to reconcile with an upset child, we must always ask, 'May I hug you?', 'May I kiss you?' If the child refuses, you must respect his wish but you should say, 'Please consider yourself hugged or kissed by me.' By saying this you will have created an imaginary loving gesture.

In the case of Thomas, it was especially important to set boundaries for demonstrated affection, as he had body issues. Thomas was burned as a toddler and in the context of the extensive medical procedures that he underwent, his body boundaries were constantly violated. As a result, he could not maintain a healthy distance towards his own body and the bodies of others.

The third session – parental presence

The kindergarten teacher has said that Thomas's frequent crises have decreased to about one a day. The parents also reported that they had an excellent week.

NON-VIOLENT RESISTANCE TECHNIQUES

- *Keeping Thomas in mind:* Dad, who works till the late evening hours will start to make daily calls home from work. The aim is to say, 'Hello, I am thinking of you and I am here! I am at work, but I am thinking of you.'

- *Leisure time:* Dad will also spend one hour with Thomas, not necessarily at home, on a designated day each week. Dad is also asked to come up with an idea for a fun activity he can undertake with Thomas at this time.

The fourth session – the initial change

The parents arrived at the meeting excited and sounded very encouraged by events. Dad told about his experience of his first trip with Thomas in his entire life. The success of the trip has generated a strong feeling of fondness towards his son – a feeling, he claimed, he had never experienced in his entire relationship with Thomas. The daily chats from work were gradually becoming easier and making more sense. Although Dad was initially uneasy about these calls, this interaction has begun to bear fruit – it seemed that both Thomas and his elder brother are pleased to speak to their Dad.

Mum said that she and Thomas are now able to visit friends because Thomas can play without any need for her intervention, and without her having to protect the other children.

At the end of the meeting the parents decided to celebrate their progress by having a meal with their relatives.

NON-VIOLENT RESISTANCE TECHNIQUES

- *Respecting personal space*: Members of the family that are usually very loving, like Thomas's grandparents, will also ask permission before hugging and kissing him.

The last session – celebrating change

Thomas's parents arrived relaxed but expressed their concern about losing the support of the therapy team. They do not report any incidents involving Thomas's excessive behaviour. Dad has brought Thomas to kindergarten without any incidents and there are many 'tantrum free' mornings. On other mornings, the parents have managed to intercept the signs of trouble and have calmed Thomas down. At the special Friday dinner they planned in the last session, the family gathered in a restaurant and the planned ceremony took place. Grandfather said the blessing with the wine and added a special blessing for Thomas. This was followed in turn by each other family member present congratulating Thomas and his family on their new way.

The parents reported that Thomas's self-destructive speech had stopped altogether and that Thomas's habit of banging his head against the wall had also stopped. Thomas had started to ask permission to hug and kiss them. The parents have also begun to ask permission before hugging and kissing Thomas and saw to it that the grandparents did likewise. According to the kindergarten teacher, there is also improvement in class. In spite of some occasions where Thomas had to be told off, no serious incidents had taken place. At kindergarten Thomas's self-destructive expressions have reduced considerably and Thomas was not disturbing the other kids nearly as often as he used to, and was getting along much better with the other children.

Dad was particularly excited about his new involvement at home and by his ability to set the tone and offer options without 'threatening' his children. In the morning, when he is responsible for bringing Thomas to kindergarten, Thomas presents himself proudly to his Dad: fully dressed and exclaiming 'I'm ready!' In the past week, as is customary in the kindergarten, Dad stayed to play with Thomas and the kids gathered around to cheer Thomas to victory. The parents are invited (but not obligated) to spend some time with the kids every morning. This is not restricted to specific days, but takes place every morning between 7:15am and 8:30am, before the formal program begins.

Thomas demonstrated great difficulties playing social games in which he could lose. Each time he lost, he would throw a major tantrum. His father, too, was a person who could not bear to lose a game, even to his son, so it was an excellent opportunity for father and son to exercise losing and winning, as well as playing for its own sake. Thomas's father began not only to accompany his son to kindergarten, but also to participate in activities that he had been unwilling to, prior to this time. For this reason, the kids cheered for Thomas. This spontaneous cheer was a visible, tangible sign of Thomas's progress.

The father keeps repeating that he never imagined it to be so easy. He tells the team that he wants to organize a family trip, something that the family did not dare do in the past, in order to 'build a common past and family experiences that we do not have'.

Thomas remains a challenging child. It is important to stay calm as his parents and teachers without losing nerve. Although Thomas still complains sometimes, it is much easier to talk to him now than to the child who shouted, 'I deserve to die'.

7749768R00055

Printed in Germany
by Amazon Distribution
GmbH, Leipzig